Meatloaf Recipes

Top 50 Most Delicious Meatloaf Recipes

By

Nancy Kelsey

Nancy Kelsey

ISBN-13:978-1512234800

ISBN-10:151223480X

DISCLAIMER

Table of Content:

Turkey Meatloaf

- **Total Preparation & Cooking Time:** 1 hr& 5 mins
- **Servings: 5**

Ingredients:

- 2 tablespoons butter (or margarine)
- 1 cup onion, chopped
- 3 cloves garlic, minced
- 1 1/4 lbs ground turkey
- 1/2 cup breadcrumbs
- 1 egg (or 1/4 cup egg substitute)
- 3/4 cup catsup
- 2 teaspoons Worcestershire sauce
- 3/4 teaspoon salt
- 1/2 teaspoon black pepper

Cooking Directions:

1. Take a large skillet or a wok and melt the butter in it.
2. Cook garlic and onion in the melted butter (stirring occasionally) approximately 5 to 6 minutes.
3. Transfer the mixture in a large bowl and let it cool approximately 5 to 7 minutes.
4. With the onion mixture, mix together the egg, bread crumbs, turkey, Worcestershire sauce, 1/4 cup of the catsup, pepper, and salt.
5. Press the meatloaf into a loaf pan (8x4").

6. Spread the leftover catsup over the top.
7. Bake in a preheated oven at 175C/350 F approximately an hour or so (the internal temperature of the turkey should reach 165 F.).

Variations:

- You may use whole wheat bread crumbs & instead of using ketchup, you may use small can of tomato sauce (approximately 8oz.).
- You may even use Panko breadcrumbs

Brown Sugar Meatloaf

- **Total Preparation & Cooking Time: 1 hr& 20 mins**
- **Servings: 8**

Ingredients

- ½ cup brown sugar, packed
- ½ cup ketchup
- 1 ½ lbs lean ground beef
- ¾ cup milk
- 2 eggs
- 1 ½ teaspoons salt
- ¼ teaspoon ground black pepper
- 1 small onion, chopped

- ¼ teaspoon ground ginger
- ¾ cup saltine crumbs, finely crushed

Cooking Directions

1. Preheat the oven at 175C/350 F.
2. Slightly grease a loaf pan (5x9").
3. In the bottom of the prepared loaf pan, add brown sugar &spread the ketchup over it.
4. Thoroughly mix all of the leftover ingredients in a mixing bowl &formthe mixture into a loaf.
5. Place the loaf over the top of the ketchup.
6. Bake in the already preheated oven until juices are clear, approximately an hour.

Variations:

- Instead of using the ketchup you may use salsa.
- Instead of using ketchup, you may use Picante sauce, and instead of saltines, you may ritz the crackers.

Meatloaf Barbecue Style

- **Total Preparation & Cooking Time: 1 hr& 30 mins**
- **Servings: 6**

Ingredients:

- 1 ½ lbs ground beef
- ½ cup fresh breadcrumb
- 1 onion, finely chopped
- 1 egg, beaten
- 1 ½ teaspoons salt
- 1 (8 ounce) can tomato sauce
- ¼ teaspoon pepper
- ½ cup water
- 3 tablespoons brown sugar
- 2 tablespoons prepared mustard
- 2 teaspoons Worcestershire sauce

Cooking Directions:

1. Combine the crumbs, beef, egg, onion, pepper, salt and half can of tomato sauce together.
2. Shape into loaf & place the loaf into a loaf pan.
3. Combine all of the leftover ingredients and transfer the mixture over the loaf.
4. Bake in 175C/350F oven approximately 1 hour &and 15 minutes.

Variations:

- During the last half hour of baking, you may add some grated cheese to the top.
- You may add only one tbsp. of brown sugar.

Crock Pot Meatloaf

- *Total Preparation & Cooking Time: 7 hrs& 15 mins*
- *Servings: 6*

Ingredients

- 2 beaten eggs
- 3⁄4 cup milk
- 2⁄3 cup fine dry breadcrumb
- 2 tablespoons grated onions
- 1 teaspoon salt
- 1⁄2 teaspoon ground sage
- 1 1⁄2 lbs lean ground beef

Sauce

- *1⁄4 cup catsup*
- *2 tablespoons brown sugar*
- *1 teaspoon dry mustard*
- *1⁄4 teaspoon ground nutmeg*

Cooking Directions:

1. Mix together the meat with eggs, milk, onion, bread crumbs, sage, and salt.
2. Shape the mixture into a 9x5" loaf.
3. Oval or rectangle.

4. Place the loaf carefully into a slow cooker.
5. Cover; cook on low settings approximately 6 to 7 hours.
6. Now, mix together the sauce ingredients and transfer over the meat loaf &cook on high approximately 15 more minutes.

Variations:

- Added green pepper and pepper (chopped) to your meatloaf.
- You may also add a few potatoes after wrapping them in a foil

<u>Cheddar Meatloaf</u>

- Total Preparation & Cooking Time: 2 hrs& 10 mins
- Servings: 7

Ingredients:-

- 2 lbs ground beef
- 1 1/2 cups Italian breadcrumbs (or plain)
- 0.75 (16 ounce) jar mild salsa
- 1/4 cup ketchup

- ½ cup cheddar cheese or ½ cup mozzarella cheese, small diced
- 2 dashes basil
- 2 dashes oregano
- 2 dashes onion powder
- 2 dashes garlic powder
- 1 pinch salt
- 1 pinch pepper
- 1 egg
- shredded cheese, for the top

Cooking Directions :-

1. Mix together everything but don't mix the shredded cheese.
2. Shape the mixture into a loaf pan.
3. Spread a small layer of ketchup over the top.
4. Bake at 190C/375 F approximately 1 hr and 30 minutes, top with cheese. Bake again until cheese completely melts. Cover the top with foil, if looks too cooked and decrease the heat to 175C/350F.

Variations:

- You may use 6 halved green olives.
- You may even replace the ketchup with salsa and top with cheese.

Meatloaf with Pineapple Topping

- **Total Preparation & Cooking Time: 1 hr& 15 mins**
- **Servings: 6**

Ingredients

- 1 ½ lbs ground beef
- 1 cup crushed Ritz cracker
- ⅓ cup milk
- ¼ cup chopped onion
- ¼ cup ketchup
- 1 tablespoon Worcestershire sauce
- 1 egg
- ½ teaspoon salt
- ⅛ teaspoon pepper

Sauce

- 1 (8 1/4 ounce) can crushed pineapple, undrained
- ½ cup ketchup
- 2 tablespoons brown sugar
- 2 teaspoons cornstarch

Cooking Directions:

1. Mix all of the meatloaf ingredients together.
2. Form the mixture into loaf (9x4) in an ungreased pan (13x9).
3. Bake at 175C/350Fapproximately 50 minutes.

4. Mix all of the sauce ingredients together in a saucepan.
5. Over medium heat settings, cook until thickens and starts boiling,stirring frequently.
6. Spread the sauce over the top of the loaf and bake for 15 to 20 more minutes.
7. Let the loaf to stand approximately 5 minutes just before slicing.

Variations:

- You may cook the onions in advance and then add some fresh garlic (that you need to cook)
- For the sauce, you may use 1 tbsp. of brown sugar

Barbecue Meatloaf

- **Total Preparation & Cooking Time: 45 mins**
- **Servings: 4**

Ingredients

- 1 lb 93% lean ground beef
- 1/2 cup barbecue sauce, divided
- 1/4 cup frozen chopped onions, pressed dry
- 1/4 cup Italian seasoned breadcrumbs
- 2 large egg whites

Cooking Directions

1. Preheat the oven at 190C/375F.
2. In a large bowl, mix together the meat, egg whites, onion, 1/4 cup barbecue sauce, breadcrumbs, &seasons of your liking and stir well.
3. Form the mixture into a loaf pan. Spread the leftover barbecue sauce at the top of the loaf.
4. Bake at 190C/375F until it reaches your desired doneness, approximately 40 to 50 minutes.

Variations:

- You may use a muffin tin, if you don't want to use BBQ.
- You may even use 96% leaner ground beef.

Meatloaf Muffins

- Total Preparation & Cooking Time: 45 mins
- Servings: 8

Ingredients

- 1 (6 ounce) box Stove Top stuffing mix
- 2 eggs
- 1 cup water

- 2 lbs ground beef or 2 lbs turkey

Cooking Directions

1. Mix everything together in a large bowl.
2. Use cooking spray to spray the muffin tins, esp.for the turkey.
3. Fill the muffins tins till top.
4. Bake at 175C/350F approximately half an hour.

Variations:

- You may cut the recipe in half and may use ground turkey, ketchup and Worcestershire sauce.
- You may even serve it with garlic green beans, garlic mashed potatoes brown gravy.

Crock Pot Meatloaf

- Total Preparation & Cooking Time: 8hrs & 15 mins
- Servings: 4

Ingredients

- 1 egg
- 1/4 cup milk

- 2 slices bread, cubed day old
- 1/4 onion, finely chopped
- 2 tablespoons finely chopped green peppers
- 1 teaspoon salt
- 1/4 teaspoon pepper
- 1 1/2 lbs lean ground beef
- 1/4 cup ketchup
- 8 medium carrots, peeled and cut in 1 inch chunks
- 8 small red potatoes

Cooking Directions:

1. Beat egg &milk in a medium size bowl.
2. Stir in green pepper, onion, bread cubes, pepper and salt.
3. Put the pieces of beef in the mixture & combine well.
4. Form into a round loaf.
5. Place the loaf in a Crock Pot (5 qt).
6. Spread the ketchup over the top of the loaf.
7. Place carrots nearby the loaf in the Crockpot.
8. Peel a strip nearby every potato & arrange potatoes over the carrots.
9. Cover; cook on high settings approximately an hour. Decrease the heat to LOW settings. Cover; cook on low settings until vegetables are tender, and meat is no longer pink, approximately 7 to 8 hours.

Variations:

- You may even brush the red potatoes and carrots with butter & may put in some dried parsley
- You may even add a small quantity of the Worchester sauce to the meat mix

---

<u>Cranberry & Turkey Meatloaf</u>

- Total Preparation & Cooking Time: 1hr & 5 mins
- Servings: 6

Ingredients

- 1 1/2 lbs ground turkey
- 1 (120 g) box turkey stuffing mix
- 2 eggs
- 1/3 cup milk or 1/3 cup water
- 1/2 cup onion, diced
- 1/2 cup celery, diced
- 1/2 cup dried cranberries

Cooking Directions

1. In a large bowl, mix together everything and combine well.
2. Transfer the mixture to a loaf pan (already greased).
3. Bake uncovered in a preheated oven at 350 F/175C approximately an hour.

4. Remove the loaf from the heat & before slicing, allow it to rest approximately 10 minutes at room temperature.

Variations

- You may omit the water/milk and may use one cup of whole cranberry sauce, homemade.
- You may leave cranberries.

Gyro Loaf With Tsatziki Sauce

- Total Preparation & Cooking Time: 2hr & 20 mins
- Servings: 8

Ingredients

For Gyro Loaf
- 1 lb ground lamb
- 1 lb ground beef
- 1 teaspoon oregano
- 1 1/2 tablespoons onion powder
- 1 tablespoon garlic powder
- 3/4 tablespoon ground pepper
- 1 teaspoon thyme
- 3/4 teaspoon salt
- 1/8 teaspoon cinnamon
- 1/8 teaspoon allspice

Tsatziki Sauce

- 1 cup sour cream
- 1 medium cucumber, grated & squeezed dry
- ½ teaspoon garlic powder
- ½ teaspoon salt
- 1 tablespoon parsley
- ¼ teaspoon dill

Cooking Directions

1. Mix together the meat loaf ingredients &shape the mixture into a loaf (freeform) in a baking pan.
2. Bake at 190C/375F approximately 75 mins.
3. Slice the loaf as thin as possible, once the loaf has cooled at room temperature (maximum of ¼").
4. Serve it at room temperatureorwarm.
5. You can serve this meatloaf with pitas, tortillas or flatbreads with tomato, lettuce, feta cheese, Tsatziki Sauce &black olives or with a potato salad, Greek salad, orpasta salad.

Variations:

- You may use 1/2 buffalo & 1/2 beef
- You may even use turkey, ground

Easy Pleasing Meatloaf

- Total Preparation & Cooking Time: 1hr & 20 mins
- Servings: 8

Ingredients

- 1 cup water
- 2 lbs lean ground beef
- ½ cup onion, finely diced
- 1 (6 1/4 ounce) package Stove Top stuffing mix
- 2 eggs
- ½ cup ketchup, divided

Cooking Directions

1. In a large bowl, combine everything together but keep 1/4 cup of ketchup for later use.
2. Shape the mixture to loaf.
3. Place the loaf in a baking dish (9x13 inch).
4. Top the loaf with the leftover ketchup.
5. Bake at 375 F/190C approximately an hour.

Variations

- You may try adding green peppers.

- You may also use ground turkey.

Turkey Meatloaf

- Total Preparation & Cooking Time: 1hr & 10 mins
- Servings: 4

Ingredients

- 1 lb ground turkey breast
- ⅓ cup quick-cooking oats
- ¼ cup nonfat milk
- 1 egg, beaten
- ⅓ cup chili sauce
- 1 small onion, finely chopped
- 1 small red pepper, finely chopped
- 1 tablespoon Worcestershire sauce
- salt and pepper
- ketchup

Cooking Directions

1. Mix the milk and oats together in a small bowl and let the oats absorb the milk approximately 10 minutes.
2. In a large bowl, combine together everything (don't add the ketchup) and absorbed oats.
3. Using large fork, combine everything and mix well.

4. Using cooking spray, spray a baking pan (9x13 inch).
5. Shape the mixture into loaf& brush it with ketchup.
6. Bake at 175C/350 F approximately 50 mins. Serve warm and enjoy.

Variations

- Before adding the pepper and onions to the mixture, you may sauté it first. Before adding this sautéed mixture to the other ingredients, you would have to cool it down.
- You may even add a large clove of minced garlic.

Meatloaf Muffins

- Total Preparation & Cooking Time: 25 mins
- Servings: 4

Ingredients

- 1 lb ground beef
- 1 egg
- *1/2 cup breadcrumbs*
- *1/2 packet onion soup mix*
- *barbecue sauce*

Cooking Directions

1. Using your hands, mix everything but don't add the sauce.
2. Distribute evenly into jumbo cups of muffin tin.
3. Transfer the barbeque sauce on each muffin's top.
4. Bake at 175C/350F approximately 20 mins.
5. Serve with cheese and mac or mashed potatoes.

Variations

- For a little spicy twist, you may add some of the chorizo to the ground beef
- If you don't have the BBQ sauce with you, you may always substitute a squirt of ketchup, a sprinkle of Costco's mesquite seasoning blend and a splash of Worcestershire sauce.

Diner Meatloaf Muffins

- Total Preparation & Cooking Time: 35 mins
- Servings: 6

Ingredients

- 1 teaspoon olive oil
- 1 cup finely chopped onion

- ½ cup finely chopped carrot
- 1 teaspoon dried oregano
- 2 garlic cloves, minced
- 1 cup ketchup, divided
- 1 ½ lbs extra lean ground beef (raw)
- 1 cup finely crushed saltine crackers (about 20)
- 2 tablespoons prepared mustard
- 1 teaspoon Worcestershire sauce
- ¼ teaspoon fresh ground black pepper
- 2 large eggs
- cooking spray

Cooking Directions

1. Preheat your oven at 350F/175C.
2. Over medium-high settings in a large nonstick skillet, heat the olive oil. Add chopped carrot, chopped onion, minced garlic and dried oregano; sauté approximately two mins and then let it cool for some time.
3. Except cooking spray, in a large bowl, combine together 1/2 cup ketchup, onion mixture, and the leftover ingredients.
4. Using cooking spray, coat 12 muffin cups and spoon the mixture into them. Top each cup with two tsp. of ketchup. Bake at 175C/350Funtil a thermometer registers 160F, approximately half an hour. Let it stand approximately 5 minutes.

Variations

- Rather than using salt, extra garlic, you may use 1/2 gr. turkey sausage and 1/2 gr. turkey (2 pounds total) and may omit the black pepper.
- You may double the veggies and may use 1/2 Ketchup, 1/2 BBQ sauce and may use ground turkey.

Cracker Barrel Meatloaf

- *Total Preparation & Cooking Time: 1hr & 5 mins*
- *Servings: 9*

Ingredients

- 2 eggs
- 2/3 cup milk
- 32 Ritz crackers, crushed
- 1/2 cup chopped onion
- 4 ounces shredded sharp cheddar cheese
- 1 teaspoon salt
- 1/4 teaspoon pepper
- 1 1/2 lbs ground beef
- 1/2 cup ketchup
- 1/2 cup brown sugar
- 1 teaspoon mustard

Cooking Directions

1. Preheat your oven at 350F/175C.
2. Beat the eggs in a large bowl and add crackers and milk. Stir in cheese and onion and then add the ground beef. Combine the ingredients well and shape the mixture into a loaf.
3. Bake at 175C/350 F approximately 45 mins.
4. To make topping, combine brown sugar, mustard and ketchup. After half an hour of baking, spoon half of the topping over the meatloaf. Return the loaf to oven and bake approximately 10 mins more. Spoon the leftover topping over the meatloaf and return it to the oven &bake approximately 5mins more.

Variations

- You may also add a dash of garlic powder, chopped green peppers, pepper and salt to the meat and may also add approximately a dash or two of Worcestershire sauce and 1/4 cup of Sweet Baby Ray's BBQ sauce to the topping and broil at the end to caramelize the sauce.
- You may serve this recipe with steamed broccoli and garlic mashed potatoes.

Quaker Oats Meatloaf

- Total Preparation & Cooking Time: 1hr & 15 mins
- Servings: 6

Ingredients

- 2 lbs ground beef
- 1 cup tomato sauce or 1 cup ketchup or 1 cup salsa
- 3/4 cup Quaker Oats
- 1/2 cup chopped onion
- 1 large egg, beaten
- 1 tablespoon soy sauce or 1 tablespoon Worcestershire sauce
- salt and pepper

Cooking Directions

1. Preheat your oven at 350F/175C and mix everything together.Shape the mixture into loaf and put in loaf pan &bake approximately an hour.
2. Drain the excess fat off from the loaf and add 2 eggs and 2/3 cup milk and bake for some more time.

Variations

- You may even add green peppers.
- Serve this with cooked rice.

Easy And Tasty Meatloaf

- Total Preparation & Cooking Time: 55 mins
- Servings: 7

Ingredients

- 1 lb ground beef
- 2 tablespoons dry onion soup mix
- 1 (5 ounce) can evaporated milk (2/3 cup)
- 2 tablespoons ketchup
- 2 tablespoons firmly packed brown sugar
- 1 teaspoon mustard

Cooking Directions

1. Preheat your oven at 350 F/175C.
2. Combine beef, onion soup mix & evaporated milk in loaf pan (8x4 Inch); mix well. Press evenly in the pan.
3. In a small bowl, mix the ketchup, mustard, and brown sugar together and spoon over the mixture.
4. Bake approximately 45 mins.
5. Lift the meat loaf from the pan to a serving plate using spatulas. Serve warm & enjoy!

Variations

- Instead of using evaporated milk, you may even use 2% milk.
- You may even use an entire packet of dry onion soup mix (approximately 3 tablespoon) and may triple the topping.

Salsa Meatloaf (OAMC)

- Total Preparation & Cooking Time: 50 mins
- Servings: 1

Ingredients
For Loaf

- 1 lb ground beef
- 3/4 cup breadcrumbs or 3/4 cup cracker crumbs or 3/4 cup oatmeal
- 1 small onion, diced
- 1 tablespoon Worcestershire sauce
- 1/2 package dry onion soup mix
- 1 egg
- 1 teaspoon garlic
- 1/2 teaspoon pepper
- 3/4 cup salsa

For Sauce

- 3/4 cup salsa
- 1 teaspoon brown sugar

- 1 teaspoon chili powder
- 2 tablespoons ketchup

Cooking Directions

1. For loaf, mix the loaf ingredients together &place the mixture in a loaf pan.
2. Bake at 175C/350 F until almost done, approximately 45 minutes.
3. Top the loaf with sauce &bake 10 to 15 more minutes.
4. For OAMC: Complete the 1 & 2 step but bake until done. Defrost the mixture overnight, top it with sauce &then bake at 175C/350 F until sauce bubbles, approximately 20 minutes.

Variations

- If you don't use the onion soup mix and onion, you may always substitute some dried onion flakes.
- You may even use the whole package of dry onion soup mix.

Ground Beef Meatloaf

- Total Preparation & Cooking Time: 1 hr& 40 mins
- Servings: 6

Ingredients

- 1 1/2 lbs ground beef
- 1 cup cracker crumb
- 1 1/4 teaspoons salt
- 1/4 teaspoon pepper
- 1 large egg, beaten
- 1 medium onion, chopped
- 1/2 cup tomato sauce

For Topping

- 3/4 cup ketchup
- 2 tablespoons firmly packed brown sugar
- 1 cup water
- 2 tablespoons mustard
- 2 tablespoons vinegar

Cooking Directions

1. Preheat the oven at 325 F/160C.
2. Mix together the cracker crumbs, ground beef, pepper, salt, tomato sauce, onion and egg in a large mixing bowl.
3. Mix very lightly.
4. Shape the mixture into loaf &place it in a baking dish.
5. Combine ketchup, water, brown sugar, vinegar and mustard in a small mixing bowl.

Nancy Kelsey

6. Brush this mixture on top of the loaf.
7. Arrange the meat loaf in an oven &bake basting occasionally with sauce, approximately 75 mins.

Variations:

- You may use tomato paste mixed with a small quantity of water, if you don't want to use tomato sauce.
- You may make these meatballs without the onions and used half of the water in the sauce.

Vegetarian Meatloaf

- *Total Preparation & Cooking Time: 1 hr& 20 mins*
- *Servings: 8*

Ingredients

- 1 (16 ounce) carton cottage cheese
- 4 eggs, beaten
- 1/4 cup vegetable oil
- 1 (1 ounce) envelope dry onion soup mix
- 1 cup finely chopped walnuts
- 1 1/2-2 1/2 cups corn flakes

34

- 1/4 cup chopped onion

Cooking Directions

1. Preheat the oven at 175 C/350 F and grease a loaf pan.
2. Mix together the eggs, walnuts, cottage cheese, soup mix, vegetable oil, onion and cereal in a large bowl.
3. Spoon the mixture into the prepared pan and bake approximately 75 mins.
4. Allow the 'roasted loaf' to rest approximately 10 mins; turn out the loaf onto a serving platter.

Variations:

- You may use 1/4 cup of finely chopped walnuts, approximately 1/3 cup of ground flax seed &wheat bran
- For additional flavors, you may add about 1/3 cup ketchup, 1 to 2 tbsp. Of Worcestershire sauce, garlic, parsley, chervil and salt.

Delicious Beef Meatloaf

- *Total Preparation & Cooking Time: 1 hr& 20 mins*
- *Servings: 6*

Ingredients

- 2⁄3 cup evaporated milk, undiluted (Pet brand preferred)
- 1 egg
- 1 cup cracker crumb
- 1 ½ lbs ground beef
- ½ cup chopped onion
- 1 ½ teaspoons salt
- 1 teaspoon dry mustard

Cooking Directions

1. Mix the ingredients as per the given order and press into a greased loaf pan (8x5x3 inch).
2. Bake the mixture in oven at 175C/350F approximately an hour.
3. Before slicing, let the meat loaf to stand approximately 5 to 10 minutes.

Variations:

- You may use Panko breadcrumbs, if you don't have crackers.
- Instead of using cracker crumbs, you may use whole wheat bread crumbs.

Italian Meatloaf

- *Total Preparation & Cooking Time: 1 hr& 45 mins*
- *Servings: 8*

Ingredients

- 3 cups soft breadcrumbs
- 3/4 cup milk
- 2 teaspoons salt
- 1/4 teaspoon pepper
- 1/2 teaspoon thyme
- 3/4 teaspoon basil
- 1 (8 ounce) can tomato sauce
- 1/2 cup onion, chopped
- 2 tablespoons butter
- 2 lbs lean ground beef
- 1 cup mozzarella cheese, shredded

Cooking Directions

1. Let the bread to soak the milk.
2. Add thyme, pepper, salt, 1/4 cup tomato sauce, 1/2 tsp basil; stir & break up the bread cubes, using fork.
3. Sauté onions in butter until soft, approximately 5 minutes and then add onions to the bread mixture.

4. Lightly mix the ingredients using fork.
5. Add ground beef to the mixture & if required, mix beef with the mixture using your hands.
6. Turn the mixture into a loaf pan& bake at 175C/350F approximately an hour; then drain the excess fat.
7. Turn into shallow baking dish and mix the leftover basil and tomato sauce. Spoon the mixture at the top of the loaf and sprinkle cheese over it.Bake approximately 15 minutes more. Serve warm & enjoy!

Variations:

- For mini meatloaves, put the meat into a muffin pan.
- You may use some dried minced onions and omit the mozzarella.

Cheese Stuffed Italian Meatloaf

- Total Preparation & Cooking Time: 1 hr& 10 mins
- Servings: 8

Ingredients

- 1 egg
- 1 cup seasoned dry bread crumb

- 1 teaspoon minced garlic
- 1/2 cup of your favorite pasta sauce, homemade or in the jar
- 1 cup chopped onion
- 1/4 cup chopped fresh basil
- 3/4 lb lean ground beef
- 1/2 lb hot Italian sausage
- 1 cup cubed mozzarella cheese, in about 1/4 inch pieces
- additional pasta sauce, for garnish

Cooking Directions

1. Preheat the oven at 350 F/175C.
2. Stir together the 1/2 cup pasta sauce, egg, garlic, and breadcrumbs in a large bowl until all set.
3. Add the leftover ingredients (don't add the ones that are for garnish), and combine with the previous mixture.
4. Transfer the mixture to a large loaf pan andgarnish/top with more pasta sauce. Bake at 175C/350 F approximately an hour.
5. Serve with scalloped potatoes, spaghetti, or rice.

Variations:

- You may also use Mozzarella Cheese, fresh.

- If you like a little firmer texture to your meatloaf then you may try it without the pasta sauce on top.
-

Low-Carb Meatloaf

- *Total Preparation & Cooking Time: 1 hr& 10 mins*
- *Servings: 6*

Ingredients

- 1 1/2 lbs ground beef
- 1 cup pork rind, crumbs
- 1 egg
- 1/3 cup tomato sauce
- 1/2 teaspoon salt
- 1/2 teaspoon pepper
- 2 tablespoons parsley
- 1/2 cup grated parmesan cheese
- 1/4 cup chopped onion
- 1/2 teaspoon garlic powder

Cooking Directions

1. Preheat the oven at 350 F/175C.
2. Mix everything together and shape the mixture into a firm oval loaf in shallow baking pan.
3. Bake approximately an hour and drain off the fat.

Variations:

- You may use 1/2 lbs. of pork sausage and 1 lbs. ground beef.
- You may also sprinkle some more garlic &parmesan on the top

---

Zucchini Meat Loaf

- *Total Preparation & Cooking Time: 1 hr& 05 mins*
- *Servings: 6*

Ingredients
For The Meatloaf

- 2 eggs, slightly beaten
- 2 cups zucchini, shredded
- 1 cup plain breadcrumbs
- 1/3 cup onion, chopped
- 1 teaspoon salt
- 1/2 teaspoon oregano leaves, dried
- 1/4 teaspoon pepper
- 1 1/2 lbs ground beef

For The Glaze

- 1 tablespoon brown sugar, packed

- 2 tablespoons ketchup
- 1/8 teaspoon ground ginger
- 1/8 teaspoon cumin

Cooking Directions

1. Preheat the oven at 350 F/175C.
2. Mix all of the meatloaf ingredients together in a large bowl until well blended and then press the mixture to an deep dish glass pie plate, ungreased (9 1/2 inch).
3. Bake approximately half an hour.
4. In the meantime, mix all of the topping ingredients well in a small bowl.
5. Remove meatloaf from the oven after half an hour &pour the topping over the meatloaf, spread evenly.
6. Put the meatloaf again to oven& bake until a meat thermometer displays 160 F, and thoroughly cooked in center, for 15 more minutes.
7. Before serving, let the meatloaf to stand approximately 5 minutes.

Variations:

- You may use homemade bread crumbs, gluten free.
- To cut down the fat, you may use half ground turkey& half ground beef.

Pizza Style Meatloaf

- *Total Preparation & Cooking Time: 1 hr& 15 mins*
- *Servings: 8*

Ingredients

- 2 lbs lean ground beef
- 1 (700 ml) jargarden-style low-carb pasta sauce, divided
- 1/2 cup green pepper, chopped
- 1/2 cup quick-cooking oats
- 1 cup shredded part-skim mozzarella cheese, divided
- 2 eggs, lightly beaten
- salt and pepper
- 1/2 cup chopped onion

Cooking Directions

1. Preheat the oven at 350F/175C. Combine together the 1/2 cup oats, eggs, 1/2 cup cheese, 1/2 cup green peppers, 1 cup sauce, ground beef, pepper and salt in a large bowl.
2. Shape the mixture into a loaf in a baking pan (13 x 9 inch).
3. Top the meatloaf with half cup of sauce.
4. Bake approximately 50 minutes, uncovered.

5. Top with half cup of cheese & then bake for 10 more minutes.
6. Before serving, let the meatloaf to stand approximately 10 minutes.
7. Put the meatloaf to a serving platter &serve with sauce.

Variations:

- You may also use 1.5 pounds of ground beef, but, you need to adjust the ingredients accordingly. You need to add a bit of garlic salt &1 teaspoon of Italian seasoning.
- You may also add 1/2 tbsp.of Italian seasoning or more to it.

Awesome and Healthy Meatloaf

- Total Preparation & Cooking Time: 1 hr
- Servings: 4

Ingredients

- 1 small zucchini (chopped finely)
- 1/2 of a yellow onion (chopped finely)
- 1/2 of a red bell pepper (chopped finely)

- 3 garlic cloves (chopped finely)
- 1 teaspoon salt
- 3 dashes pepper
- 1 teaspoon dried thyme
- ½ teaspoon dried oregano
- ½ teaspoon dried basil
- cooking spray
- 1 lb lean ground beef
- 1 egg
- 1 teaspoon salt
- ¼ teaspoon pepper
- 1 (8 ounce) can tomato sauce with basil garlic and oregano (divided)

Cooking Directions

1. Use cooking spray to spray a skillet.
2. Put zucchini, yellow onion, red bell pepper, garlic cloves, salt, dashes pepper, dried thyme, dried oregano & dried basil in the skillet&sauté on medium heat approximately 10 minutes. Let it cool down at room temperature.
3. Mix together the egg, ground beef, pepper, salt, the vegetable mixture and ½ of the tomato sauce in a large bowl.
4. Pat into small meatloaves (approximately seven) &place loafs on a foil lined baking sheet (already sprayed with the cooking spray).
5. Top every loaf with the leftover tomato sauce & bake at 175C/350F approximately half an hour. Serve warm & enjoy!

Variations:

- You may reduce the quantity of zucchini as per your likings.
- You may even use fresh herbs from your garden and use the ground turkey.

Maple Sage Meatloaf

- *Total Preparation & Cooking Time: 1 hr& 30 mins*
- *Servings: 6*

Ingredients

- 1 ½ lbs ground chuck
- ¾ cup sour cream
- 1 large egg
- ½ cup chopped onion
- 2 tablespoons dried parsley
- 1 teaspoon salt
- ½ teaspoon ground sage
- ¼ cup ketchup (or chili sauce)
- 2 tablespoons maple syrup (or brown sugar)
- 1 teaspoon prepared mustard
- 1 tablespoon barbecue sauce

Cooking Directions

1. Using your hands, mix together the ground chuck, sour cream, egg, onion, parsley, salt & ground sage until thoroughly mixed (before mixing the chopped onion into the loaf, microwave the onion for approximately 2 minutes on High).
2. In a casserole dish, shape the mixture into a loaf-shape.
3. Combine the leftover ingredients together & then spread at the top of the loaf.
4. Bake at 175C/350F approximately 75 minutes, after 45 minutes, drain off the fat.

Variations:

- You may add approximately a handful of plain breadcrumbs & half tsp. of salt more.
- You may also add a small quantity of oatmeal.

Crock Pot Cheesy Meatloaf

- Total Preparation & Cooking Time: 8 hrs& 10 mins
- Servings: 8

Ingredients

- 18 round cheese crackers

- 1 cup shredded cheddar cheese
- 1 small onion, finely chopped
- 2 tablespoons minced green peppers
- 1/4 cup chili sauce
- 1/2 cup milk
- 2 eggs, slightly beaten
- 3/4 teaspoon salt
- 1/8 teaspoon pepper
- 2 lbs lean ground beef

Cooking Directions

1. Use a blender or rolling pin to crush the crackers.
2. Mix together the chili sauce, shredded cheddar, crushed crackers, green pepper, onion, eggs, milk, pepper, and salt in a large bowl.
3. Add the ground beef& shape the mixture into a round loaf (approximately 7-inch).
4. Place the loaf in a crock pot.
5. Cover; cook on low settings until done, approximately 8 hours.

Variations:

- In place of using the cheese crackers, you may use Goldfish snack crackers
- You may replace chili sauce with ketchup.

Easy Stove Top Stuffing Meatloaf

- Total Preparation & Cooking Time: 1 hr& 05 mins
- Servings: 6

Ingredients

- 1 1/2 lbs ground beef
- 1 (6 ounce) box Stove Top stuffing mix
- 1/2 cup water
- 2 eggs
- 1/3 cup ketchup

Cooking Directions

1. In a large bowl, mix together the ground beef, Stove Top stuffing mix, eggs & water.
2. Pat into a square pan (8x8 inch).
3. Place a very thin layer of ketchup over the top of the loaf.
4. Bake at 175C/350F approximately an hour.

Variations:

- In place of ketchup, you may also use SweetBaby Ray's BBQ sauce.
- Instead of using the water, you may use milk.

Green olive meatloaf

- Total Preparation & Cooking Time: 1 hr& 05 mins
- Servings: 5

Ingredients

- 1 lb ground turkey
- 1⁄2 cup breadcrumbs
- 1 egg, beaten
- 1 package onion soup mix
- 20 green olives, cut in half
- 1⁄2 cup ketchup

Cooking Directions

1. Preheat the oven at 350F/175C.
2. In large bowl, use your hands to mix ground turkey, breadcrumbs, egg, onion soup mix & green olives. Use cooking oil to spray a loaf pan.
3. Shape the mixture into a loaf and put the mixture into a pan.
4. Put the ketchup on &smooth so the loaf is completely covered on the top.
5. Arrange the pan on the middle rack of the oven & bake approximately 50 minutes.

Variations:

- You may useapproximately 1/3 cup of fresh & finely diced onions, and a half cup of salad olives, sliced.
- Since the olives are salty, you may reduce the quantity of the onion soup mix for less.

Leftover Meatloaf Parmesan

- Total Preparation & Cooking Time: 35 mins
- Servings: 6

Ingredients

- 4 -6 slices leftover meatloaf
- 1 (15 ounce) can tomato sauce (or your homemade stuff)
- 1 clove garlic, minced
- 2 teaspoons Italian seasoning
- 4 -6 slices mozzarella cheese

Cooking Directions

1. Place your meatloaf slices (it may touch but it should not overlap) flat on the bottom of a cooking dish (9x13 inch).

2. Mix together the garlic, tomato sauce, seasoning &pour the mixture at the top of your meatloaf.
3. Over each meatloaf slice, place a slice of cheese.
4. Bake in a 175C/350F oven until the sauce is bubbly and the cheese is browned.

Variations:

- You may serve this loaf with Amish Green Beans and egg noodles.
- Top every slice with 1 tbsp. of tomato sauce (which already has got a blend of oregano, basil, and garlic).

Leftover Meatloaf Chili

- *Total Preparation & Cooking Time: 25 mins*
- *Servings: 2*

Ingredients

- 1 1/2-2 cups leftover meatloaf
- 1/4 cup chili powder
- 1 (15 ounce) canun-drained pinto beans
- 1 (14 1/2 ounce) canun-drained diced tomatoes
- 1 cup sharp cheddar cheese, divided

Cooking Directions

1. Mix together the chili seasoning, beans, and tomatoes in a saucepan, medium sized.
2. Heat & stir until seasonings are blended well.
3. Now, gradually add the meatloaf & stir approximately 15 minutes, until meat is heated.
4. Divide the loaf into two serving bowls&top with equal quantity of cheese, if desired.

Variations:

- You may use some coriander, cumin, garlic powder and onion powder and may decrease the quantity of the chili powder by half.
- You may even add more of cumin and garlic powder.

Meatloaf With Ground Lamb

- Total Preparation & Cooking Time: 1hr & 15 mins
- Servings: 1

Ingredients

- 2 eggs
- 1/2 cup dry breadcrumbs
- 1/2 teaspoon salt

- ¼ teaspoon black pepper
- 1 lb ground beef
- 1 lb ground lamb
- 2 tablespoons olive oil
- 1 medium onion, chopped
- 4 garlic cloves, minced
- 1 teaspoon dried thyme
- 1 teaspoon dried basil
- ½ cup ketchup or ½ cup tomato paste
- 1 tablespoon Worcestershire sauce

Cooking Directions

1. Preheat your oven at 175C/350F.
2. Sauté the basil, thyme, garlic, and onion in olive oil until the onion arealmost golden and soft in a large skillet. Remove the skillet from the heat &let the mixture to cool down slightly.
3. Beat the eggs in a large bowl and add the breadcrumbs, pepper, and salt.
4. Add your cooled garlic, herbs, and onion & the meats, ground.
5. Add the ketchup and Worcestershire sauce.
6. Now, mix together everything &place the mixture in a loaf pan, already greased.
7. Bake approximately an hour.
8. Allow it to cool at room temperature approximately 5 minutes& drain the fat. Serve and enjoy.

Variations:

- You may omit the lamb
- You may sauté the herbs &vegetables first &till the time they cool down, you may mix everything else in your stand mixer. Throw the onion mixture in and gave it a whirl.

Horseradish Meatloaf

- *Total Preparation & Cooking Time: 1hr & 5 mins*
- *Servings: 8*

Ingredients

For Meatloaf

- 2 lbs ground beef
- 3/4 cup regular oats, uncooked
- 1 large onion, chopped
- 1/2 cup catsup
- 1/4 cup milk
- 2 large eggs, lightly beaten
- 1 tablespoon prepared horseradish
- 1 1/2 teaspoons salt
- 1/2 teaspoon pepper

For Sauce

- ½ cup catsup
- 3 tablespoons brown sugar
- 1 tablespoon prepared horseradish
- 2 teaspoons spicy brown mustard

Cooking Directions

1. In a large bowl, mix all of the meatloaf ingredients well. Shape the mixture into a loaf& then place in a loafpan (9x5x3 inch).
2. In a small bowl, mix together all of the sauce ingredients and stir well. Spoon ½ of the sauce mixture at the top of your meatloaf. Bake at 190C/375 F approximately 50 minutes, uncovered.
3. Spoon the left overmixture of the sauce over the meatloaf&bake for 10 more minutes. Remove the meatloaf and put to a serving platter.

Variations:

- You may serve this dish with sliced tomatoes, mashed potatoes& baby peas
- You may even use 1/2 lb. ground pork &1-1/2 lbs. ground beef

Taco Meatloaf

- *Total Preparation & Cooking Time: 1hr & 5 mins*
- *Servings: 6*

Ingredients

- 1 1/2 lbs ground beef
- 1 cup tortilla chips or 1 cup corn chips, crushed
- 1/3 cup salsa or 1/3 cup taco sauce
- 1 tablespoon taco seasoning
- 1 egg, beaten
- 1 cup cheddar cheese, shredded

Cooking Directions

1. Use your hands to mix everything in a large bowl.
2. Bake at 175C/350 F approximately an hour in a loaf pan.
3. Drain off fat &bake for one or two more minutes.

Variations:

- You may use 1/2 pound extra lean turkey and 1 pound 96/4 lean ground beef & rather than using the regular tortilla chips, you may use the baked tortilla chips.

- You may even use a burrito seasoning mix & add some of the leftover baked beans to the mix as well.

Cornbread Meatloaf

- *Total Preparation & Cooking Time: 1hr & 5 mins*
- *Servings: 6*

Ingredients

- 1 lb ground beef
- 1/2 lb sausage
- 1 egg
- 1 cup cornbread, crumbs
- 1 onion, diced
- 1/2 teaspoon salt
- 1/4 teaspoon pepper
- 1 (8 ounce) can tomato sauce
- 2 tablespoons mustard
- 2 tablespoons vinegar
- 2 tablespoons brown sugar

Cooking Directions

1. Mix together the ground beef, half cup of the tomato sauce & pepper using your hands & shape the mixture into a loaf; place the loaf into a baking dish (greased).

2. Combine together the leftover ingredients and then transfer the mixture at the top of your meatloaf.
3. Bake at 325F/160C approximately an hour, during cooking, you need to baste 3 to 4 times.

Variations:

- You may always use honey, if you don't have any brown sugar
- You may even add cooked lentils

===

Deer Meatloaf

- Total Preparation & Cooking Time: 1hr & 40 mins
- Servings: 6

Ingredients

- 1 lb ground deer meat
- 1/2 lb lean sausage meat
- 3 slices soft bread, torn into pieces
- 1/2 cup onion, chopped
- 1/4 teaspoon pepper
- 1/4 teaspoon sage
- 1/4 teaspoon garlic salt
- 1 cup milk
- 1 1/4 teaspoons salt

- 1 egg
- ½ cup bell pepper, chopped
- ¼ teaspoon dry mustard
- ¼ teaspoon celery salt
- 1 tablespoon Worcestershire sauce

Cooking Directions

1. Preheat your oven at 350F/175C.
2. Thoroughly mix all of the ingredients.
3. Bake until done, approximately one and a half hour.

Variations:

- You can always make the topping with catsup, brown sugar & mustard and bake it on during the last 15 minutes of your baking time.
- You may even omit the sausage

Quick & Easy BBQ Meatloaf

- *Total Preparation & Cooking Time: 50 mins*
- *Servings: 4*

Ingredients

- 1 lb ground beef

- ½ cup barbecue sauce
- ½ cup quick oats, uncooked
- ½ cup onion, chopped finely
- 1 egg, beaten

Cooking Directions

1. Mix together everything but don't mix barbecue sauce (approximately 1/4 cup).
2. Form the mixture into a loaf and then in a baking dish (12x8inch).
3. Bake at 190C/375F until cooked through, approximately 50 mins. Before slicing, let the loaf to stand approximately 5 minutes. Top with leftover barbecue sauce.

Variations:

- In place of onions, you may always use a packet of onion/mushroom soup mix.
- You may even replace the BBQ topping with ketchup, if you don't want it to be sweet.

Meatloaf With Raisins

- Total Preparation & Cooking Time: 1hr & 25 mins
- Servings: 16

Ingredients

- 2 lbs lean ground beef
- 2 cups crushed wheat flakes
- 4 eggs, room temperature, slightly beaten
- 1 teaspoon salt
- 1/2 teaspoon pepper
- 1 cup milk
- 3/4 cup catsup
- 2 teaspoons Worcestershire sauce
- 2 cups raisins
- 1 medium onion, diced

Cooking Directions

1. Preheat the oven at 350 F/175 C.
2. Mix together everything & shape into a shallow dome in a baking dish with sides (10 inch round).
3. Bake for a minimum period of one hour &15 minutes.

Variations:

- In place of using whole milk, you may use 2% milk.
- Or in place of milk, you may even use buttermilk.

Cajun Meatloaf

- *Total Preparation & Cooking Time: 1hr & 20 mins*
- *Servings: 8*

Ingredients

- 1 tablespoon vegetable oil
- 2 garlic cloves, finely chopped
- 1 onion, diced
- 1 carrot, diced
- 1/2 cup red bell pepper, diced
- 1 tablespoon Cajun seasoning
- 1/2 teaspoon salt
- 1/2 teaspoon ground black pepper
- 1/2 cup corn kernel
- 1 egg, beaten
- 1 1/2 cups corn chips, roughly crushed
- 1/2 cup salsa
- 1/4 cup water
- 1 lb lean ground beef
- 1 lb ground lean pork
- 1/2 cup cheddar cheese, grated
- 2 tablespoons fresh parsley, chopped

Cooking Directions

1. Heat oil on medium heat settings in a large skillet. Add Cajun seasoning, onion, garlic, red bell pepper, carrot, pepper and salt. Cook, until onion has softened, approximately 5 minutes, stirring occasionally. Add corn & continue cooking for 2 more minutes. Let the mixture to cool for some time.
2. Mix corn chips, egg, water, salsa, mixture of veggies & pork and beef in a big bowl. Spoon this mixture on a baking sheet with foil paper &shape in a 9x5" loaf. Cook in oven (preheated) at 175C/350 F approximately 80 mins. Sprinkle cheddar cheese over the top & continue cooking until internal temperature displays 170F, approximately 10 more minutes. Let the meatloaf to stand approximately 5 mins. Drain off meatloaf fat then sprinkle parsley over it.

Variations:

- You may omit onions & may use additional red bell pepper.
- You may even use a ground chicken and beef mixture.

Cheeseburger Meatloaf

• Total Preparation & Cooking Time: 1hr & 20 mins

• Servings: 4

Ingredients

- 1 lb lean ground beef
- ¾ cup uncooked regular oats
- ½ cup milk
- 2 tablespoons minced onions
- 1 -2 minced garlic clove
- 2 tablespoons minced green peppers
- 1 large egg, beaten
- 1 teaspoon Worcestershire sauce
- ½ teaspoon salt
- ¼ teaspoon dry mustard
- ¼ teaspoon pepper
- 1 (12 ounce) bottle chili sauce
- 3 packaged cheddar cheese slices, cut into 1-inch strips
- 4 -6 slices crispy bacon

Cooking Directions

1. In a large bowl, stir together ground beef, oats, milk, onions, garlic clove, green peppers, egg, Worcestershire sauce, salt & mustard until well combined. Place the in a loafpan (9x5 inch).
2. Bake at 175C/350Fapproximately 45 mins. Pour chili sauce at the top of your meat loaf&bake until meat is no longer pink in center, approximately half an hour more.

3. Place bacon on meatloaf (if using), then arrange cheese slices in a crisscross pattern over the meat loaf. Before slicing, let the loaf to stand approximately 10 minutes.

Variations:

- In place of using the slices, you may use ground round, 12 oz. of chili sauce& sharp cheddar cheese, shredded.
- You may put half cup of sharp cheddar right in the loaf and use 1 teaspoon of garlic powder.

Salsa Meatloaf

- *Total Preparation & Cooking Time: 50 mins*
- *Servings: 6*

Ingredients

- 1 lb lean ground beef or 1 lb lean ground buffalo
- 1 egg
- 1 cup rolled oats
- 1 cup salsa, from a jar, use your favorite kind

Cooking Directions

1. Thoroughly mix everything and then bake at 175C/350F approximately 45 minutes in an oiled loaf pan.

Variations:

- You may use 93% ground beef
- You may also use a hot & spicy salsa

Autumn Meatloaf

- *Total Preparation & Cooking Time: 1hr & 15 mins*
- *Servings: 12*

Ingredients

- 2 lbs ground turkey
- 1 (10 ounce) package frozen chopped spinach (thawed, drained and squeeze dry)
- 1 cup cheddar cheese, shredded
- 1/2 cup mushroom, finely chopped (optional)
- 1/2 cup red onion, chopped fine
- 4 garlic cloves, chopped
- 1 (1 1/4 ounce) envelope onion soup mix
- 2 large eggs, beaten
- 1/2 cup plain breadcrumbs
- 2 tablespoons prepared yellow mustard
- 1 tablespoon Worcestershire sauce
- 1/2 teaspoon poultry seasoning

- ½ teaspoon black pepper
- 2 cups tomato ketchup (optional)

Cooking Directions

1. Mix everything together until well combined. Place the mixture into a loaf pan, large. If desired, spread ketchup at the top of the mixture.
2. Preheat the oven at 350F/175C &bake until internal temperature displays 165F, approximately an hour. Let stand, covered approximately 10 minutes to finish cooking and to set the meatloaf (final temperature should reflect 170F).
3. Remove the loaf from the pan and place on a serving platter.

Variations:

- You may omit the mushrooms.
- For the onion soup mix, you may use Onion Seasoning Mix.

Turkey Salsa Meatloaf

- *Total Preparation & Cooking Time: 1hr & 15 mins*
- *Servings: 5*

Ingredients

- 2 eggs
- 1 cup oats
- 1 onion, minced
- 3/4 cup grated carrot
- 1 1/2 teaspoons Worcestershire sauce
- 1/2 teaspoon salt
- 2 teaspoons garlic powder
- 1/2 teaspoon dried thyme
- 1 lb ground turkey
- 1/2 cup salsa

Cooking Directions

1. Mix everything together but don't add the salsa &from into a loaf; put in the oven at 175C/350F approximately40 mins.
2. Remove the loaf from the oven; cover with salsa &bake until done, approximately half an hour more.

Variations:

- You may add a minced chipotle&a touch of cilantro
- You may omit onions and may add a small quantity of jalapeno

Meatloaf Sandwiches

- *Total Preparation & Cooking Time: 15 mins*
- *Servings: 1*

Ingredients

- ½ inch thick leftover meatloaf
- 2 slices Monterey jack cheese
- 2 slices whole grain bread
- olive oil

Cooking Directions

1. Place the slice of your meat loaf between 2 bread slices and2 cheese slices.
2. Use olive oil to brush your sandwich's outside.
3. Cook sandwich over medium low settings in skillet, turning occasionally (4 to 5 minutes each side).

Variations:

- You may put red onion (finely diced) in the sandwich
- You may even use ancient grain bread and Swiss cheese.

Turkey Meatloaf

- *Total Preparation & Cooking Time: 1hr & 20 mins*
- *Servings: 10*

Ingredients

- 1 medium onion, finely chopped
- 1 tablespoon canola oil
- 2 eggs
- 1/2 cup 2% low-fat milk
- 2 teaspoons lemon juice
- 1 teaspoon salt
- 1 teaspoon dried basil
- 1/2 teaspoon dried oregano
- 1/2 teaspoon pepper
- 2 cups whole wheat bread crumbs, soft
- 1 (10 ounce) package frozen spinach, thawed and squeezed dry
- 2 1/2 lbs lean ground turkey
- 1/2 cup salsa
- 1 tablespoon butter

Cooking Directions

1. Heat oil in a skillet& sauté the onion until tender; keep it aside.
2. Combine the lemon juice, milk, eggs, basil, salt, pepper and oregano in a large bowl. Add

the reserved onion, bread crumbsandspinach; stir to combine well. Crumble turkey over the mixture &mix until well blended.

3. Shape the mixture into a loaf (12x5-inch); place in a baking dish (13x9x2-inch) coated with cooking spray (non-sticking).Spoon salsa at the top of the loaf.

4. Bake at 175C/350F approximately half an hour, uncovered. Drizzle butter; bake until a meat thermometer reflects 165 F, for half an hour more.

Variations:

- In place of using milk, you may use rice milk and may omit the butter.
- As an alternative, you may use a packet of Lipton onion &mushroom soup mix.

Special Meatloaf With Heinz 57 Sauce

- *Total Preparation & Cooking Time: 1hr & 10 mins*
- *Servings: 6*

Ingredients

- 1 1/2 lbs lean ground beef
- 1 egg, slightly beaten

- 1 cup soft breadcrumbs
- ½ cup milk
- 6 tablespoons Heinz 57 steak sauce, divided
- 1 teaspoon salt
- ½ cup chopped onion
- 3 dashes freshly grated pepper

Cooking Directions

1. Thoroughly mix the ingredients (but reserve 3 tablespoon of Heinz 57 Sauce), make sure you don't over mix& use a light hand.
2. Shape in a loaf pan (8x4x1 ½ inches).
3. You should first grease your pan, if the ground beef is lean.
4. Brush the top of your loaf with the kept 3 tbsp.of Heinz Sauce.
5. Bake in oven at 175C/350 F approximately an hour.
6. Before slicing, let the loaf to stand approximately 5 minutes.

Variations:

- You may put approximately 6 tablespoon of the Heinz 57 in the meatloaf and approximately 3 tablespoon on the top.
- You may even add thesteak sauce and Worcestershire Sauce

Applesauce Meatloaf

- *Total Preparation & Cooking Time: 1hr & 15 mins*
- *Servings: 6*

Ingredients
For Meatloaf

- 1 lb ground beef
- 1 cup soft breadcrumbs
- 1 egg
- 2 tablespoons finely chopped onions
- 4 ounces cans applesauce
- 1 teaspoon Dijon mustard
- 1 dash pepper

For Filling

- 1/2 cup applesauce
- 1 tablespoon brown sugar
- 1 tablespoon vinegar
- 1 teaspoon Dijon mustard

Cooking Directions

1. Mix together all ofthe meatloaf ingredients &shape the mixture into a round loaf in a baking pan (8 or 9 inches).
2. In the center of the loaf, make dejection.
3. Combine all of the filling ingredients and then pour into dejection in the loaf.
4. Bake at 175C/350F approximatelyan hour.
5. Before serving, pour off the grease, if required.

Variations:

- You may add a packet of dry onion soup mix.
- You may even use applesauce, unsweetened and add 1/2 teaspoon salt to the meat mixture.

END

Conclusion

Thank you again for downloading this book!

I hope this book was able to give you the flavor that you have been looking for in your vitamin water.

The next step is to try the different recipes and share them with the people you hold dear.

Finally, if you enjoyed this book, please take the time to share your thoughts and post a review. It'd be greatly appreciated!

Thank you and good luck!

Did you enjoy this book?

I want to thank you for purchasing and reading this book. I really hope you got a lot out of it.

Can I ask a quick favor though?

If you enjoyed this book I would really appreciate it if you could leave me a positive review on Amazon.

I love getting feedback from my customers and reviews on Amazon really do make a difference. I read all my reviews and would really appreciate your thoughts.

If you have any questions, please feel free to mail me at beingpatriciabenson@yahoo.com

You can also LIKE My Facebook Page for updates and my upcoming book

Thanks so much.

Nancy Kelsey

p.s. You can click here to go directly to the book on Amazon and leave your review.

Disclaimer

THIS Book, slow cooker recipes is written with an intention to serve as purely information and educational resource. It is not intended to be a medical advice or a medical guide.

Although proper care has been taken to ensure to validity and reliability of the information provided in this book. Readers are advice to exert caution before using any information, suggestion and methods described in this book.

The writer does not advocate the use of any of the suggestion, diet and health programs mention in this book. This book is not intended to take the place of a medical profession, a doctor and physician. The information in this book should not be used without the explicit advice from medically trained professions especially in cases where urgent diagnosis and medical treatment is needed.

The author or publisher cannot e held responsible for any personal or commercial damage in misinterpreting or misunderstanding any part of the book.